BEFORE THE SUN RISES

Before the Sun Rises

45.7128938° N, 122.6878765° W

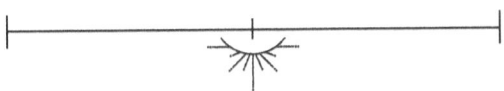

POETRY BY

GWENDOLYN MORGAN

Wayfarer
BOOKS

WAYFARER BOOKS

WWW.WAYFARERBOOKS.ORG

Published in 2019 · Homebound Publications
Published in 2024 Wayfarer Books
Front Cover Image © Susan Bourdet "Emerald Lake,"
Interior Illustrations: Crow © KHIUS · Deer
© Manekina Serafima · Rabbit © Anastasiia Firsova · Owl © InkKin
Cover and Interior Designed by Connor Wolfe
978-1-947003-45-3 / First Edition Trade Paperback
978-1-965320-03-7 / Second Edition

Due to the author's commitment to confidentiality the people and circumstances portrayed in
these poems are composite in nature. Any person or circumstance represents a combination of
many individuals and events from over two decades of spiritual care in various settings. Any
resemblance of a composite to an actual person or event is coincidental.

10 9 8 7 6 5 4 3 2

Wayfarer Books is committed to ecological stewardship.
We greatly value the natural environment and invest in conservation.

PO Box 1601, Northampton, MA 01060

wayfarer@homeboundpublications.com

WAYFARERBOOKS.ORG

ALSO BY THE AUTHOR

Crow Feathers, Red Ochre, Green Tea
Snowy Owls, Egrets and Unexpected Graces

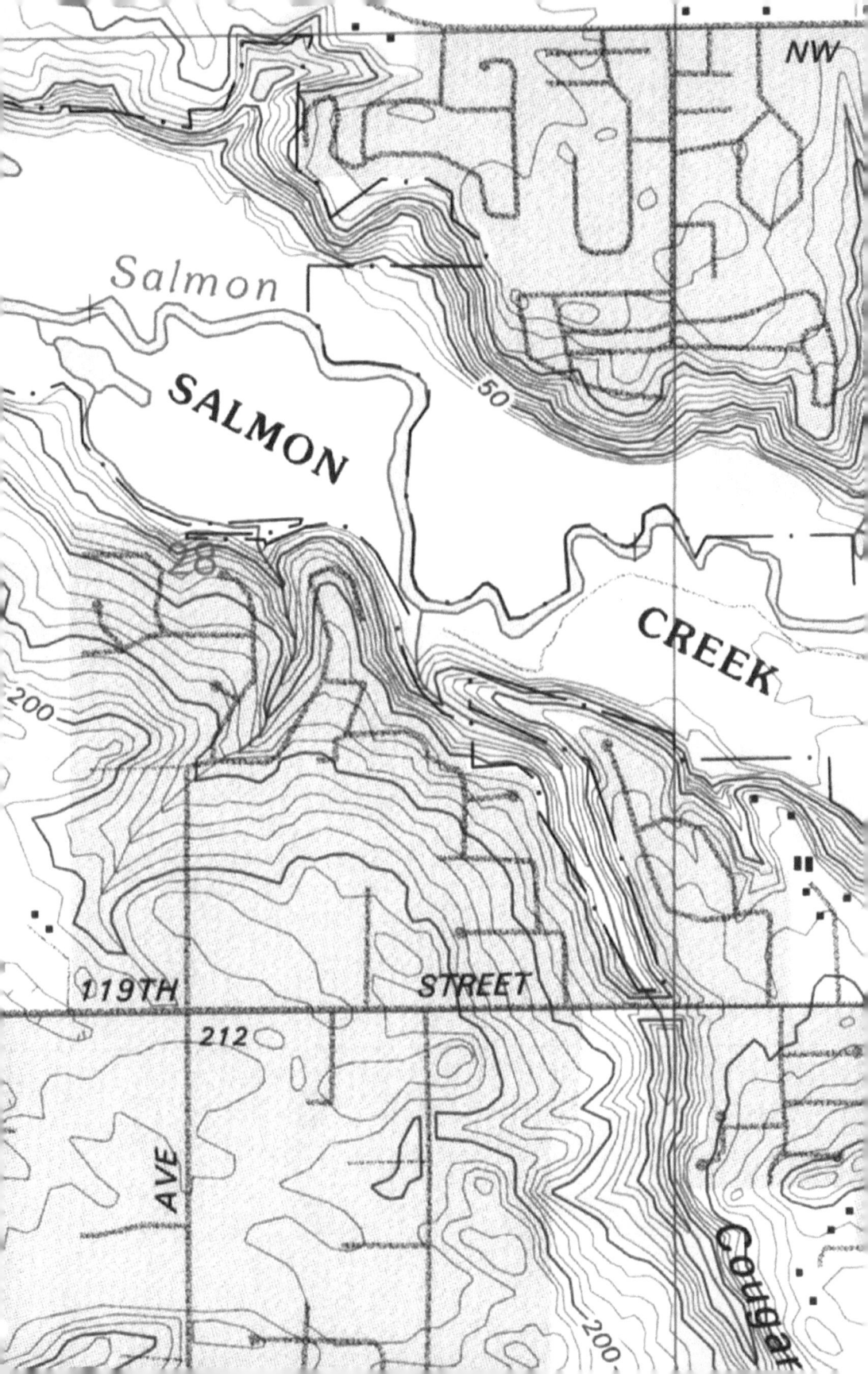

Honeybee, winged light
there's enough room in my heart
for joy, gold-leaf combs

I. CROW

II. DEER

III. ℛABBIT

IV. OWL

CROW

HOPE, EMBOSSED

Each one of us has an owl, sparrow, crow,
an ordinary bird that follows us around our home.
Kali, Ganesh, and a host of gods and goddesses,
step over the hearth. We pick up maple seed pods,
hope embossed in several languages,
yellow swallowtail, butterfly wings
ten thousand things.

BEFORE THE SUN RISES

She feeds the Northwestern Crows and the Eastern Cottontails
in her back yard. Knowing better, she breaks apart Challah,
Naan, Gluten-free whole-wheat rolls, and scatters round pieces
of organic carrots. The crows learn our faces, the timbre of
our voices, the fact that we walk our Pembroke Corgi between
four and six o'clock morning and night. They talk to us about
nearby events: the arrival of garbage and recycling trucks, feral
cats that were poisoned by our neighbors, teenagers smoking
weed in the car in the next cul-de-sac, hurried postal carriers
delivering packages. Our neighbor who is living with breast
cancer shares that she also has been feeding the crows her home-
baked sourdough bread. Then mama raccoon drags her three
babies across her lawn. She stops feeding the crows, apologizing
profusely as the baby in the family of five American Crows called
out plaintively, repeatedly, for bread. We drive our neighbor to
her next five chemotherapy appointments. She is worried about
the refugees in Europe. Red-breasted Nuthatch, Black-capped
Chickadee, Evening Grosbeak, Black-tailed Deer return more
frequently. The rabbits nibble on clover, black oil sunflower seeds,
organic carrot stubs. She listens to the spaces between *Corvid*
vocalizations, picks up Crow feathers beneath Western Red Cedar.
Three Crows, three Graces, return again and again.

NOCTURNAL

Crows wake us up
talking amongst the cedar boughs
before sunrise, before

we poured freshly ground
Kicking Horse® cliffhanger espresso
into the glass carafe

the coffee tastes like owl wings
clots of cream, brown feathers
circles of light, *kaws, kaws*

the deep green boughs of dreamtime
winds of consciousness
before the milk was warmed

on the stove, a round silver and grey sauce pan
cow milk, almond milk, goat milk
Crow told us that it was time

to set some tomato plants in to the ground
scatter wild flower seed
it would rain in the evening, after the planting

after we heard about the sacrilege on London Bridge
in Syria, Portlandia, a round of a nursery rhyme
the Max train, the wheels

a round of violence
a round of van wheels
a round knife handle

one—two—three
Crow calls three times
another, repeat, echo

repeat of gun shot
repeat of repeat of   repeat of
Crows wake us up

again in the middle of the night.
I heard "Nocturne" in my dreams,
a litany of piano keys, melodies

bells ringing in the middle of Mass
Ring the bell!
hand bell, dorje, steeple bell, when the bell rings

it signifies you have finished your treatment, chemotherapy
remission repeats, re-mission, Crow calls
when the bell rings

the sacred texts have been read
when the bell rings above the gravestone
you know you are still alive

when the bell rings, it is time for tea
for cedar, white sage, smudge stick, smoke of palo santo
a round of memory

we wonder if this is how it is
to lose memory, not remember history, the words
dancing on the edge of consciousness

Peruvian wood, santo, palo
sweet grass, repeat of forgetfulness
Crows wake us up.

AFTER CHEMOTHERAPY, MERCURY RETROGRADE NO. 2

She thought she had lost the names of the vowels in the silences between each breath, between blood draws, between cheerios of red-breasted Robins, and the infusion of Neulasta®—. She noted that with each pull and tug of earthworm, the American Robins embody patience. How small bristles allow the worm to move and burrow, this time not quickly enough. How the chemo did not act quickly enough for her friend, who was hospitalized on the first day of Mercury Retrograde, twelve days after her last treatment. How the Syrian refugees did not move their small boat quickly enough, rowing in circles in the wake of the ferry. How bodies washed up on the beaches. How this New World Thrush seemed to recognize her, look her in the eye, turn thoughtfully to the right, head tilted like her oncologist who said, "I think you'll remember." O positive blood type, blood count, Christmas bird count, border crossing count, each day counted. Slowly syllables returned to her consciousness, the wheel of the year turning toward the Angelica Blue Juniper, the wild Cosmos, the four-leaf clovers, Cedar Waxwing, consonants.
"A-E-I-O-U," she said.

SEVEN MOURNING DOVES

The seven mourning doves
gather on the ground
below the Western Red Cedar
near the potted tomato plants
the raised beds of vegetables
deciding how to announce
the weather forecast—
soft cooing, calling of rain
amidst trilliums and Oregon grape holly,
more earthquakes in Japan, Chile, the Philippines
mud slides, Syrian, African and European refugee crises
violence, bombings and mass shootings
in every country around the world.

Global upheaval
wine tasting in the neighbor's vineyard
their donkeys and cows also continue
talking about the news of
another strawberry field, farm
turned into "urban eco-housing"
Dusky Geese fly low
overhead, listening in.
The woman, her daughter and their cats,
living in a small red Volkswagen rabbit
parked near Salmon Creek trail
pick wild roses, daisies
dream of vegetable gardens.

THE SKIN OF OUR EARTH

Basal cell, squamous cell carcinoma, melanoma
troposphere, stratosphere, mesosphere
emission of green gasses
trapped near the earth's surface

solar flares, weather patterns
holes in the white layers of the atmosphere
glaciers melting faster than anesthesia
after a Mohs procedure.

Coal soaks up mercury, uranium
releases harmful minerals when burned, lung cancer
trending, the average surface temperature rising
Requiem of the great aerial ocean

pressure on climate systems, breath
Douglas Fir, evergreen trees lose their needles
grapefruit-sized hail falling on gardens
swirl, spin, undulation of tornado, tsunami

doubts of emission-reduction, Gaia
topographic map of our faces.

REKINDLING HOPE, TWANOH BEACH

i

Papyri, found in rubbish dumps in Oxyrhynchus,
fragments of Sanskrit manuscripts, from a time
when sacred stories were told around kitchen fires,
near-death experiences were understood as narratives of experience.
Like Orcas in the salt water,
our journeys rely on courage, strength, metaphor,
Sockeye Salmon, migrating upstream to spawn, anadromous hope,
Coastal Salish Red Cedar baskets filled with stone meteorites.
Perhaps we need a fjord, a palimpsest, or a new perception
of our place in this ever-changing world.

ii

Listening to our stories, the birds gather round us on the beach,
a solitary Glaucous-winged Gull waits—flies,
chased by an unleashed dog, returns.
I can hear what it is telling me.
Knowing better, I feed it crumbs of lemon pound cake,
walk to our car and retrieve chips, organic potato chips.
I apologize, wishing I had healthy alternatives.
"You're giving the seagulls the good Kettle® chips?" she asks.
Of course, the gull is hungry, thankful, it knows.
When I look in its eyes, I see its spirit. It sees mine.
Most of the eye is filled with a clear gel, the vitreous,
round mandalas of iris, midrash, pupil, stone.

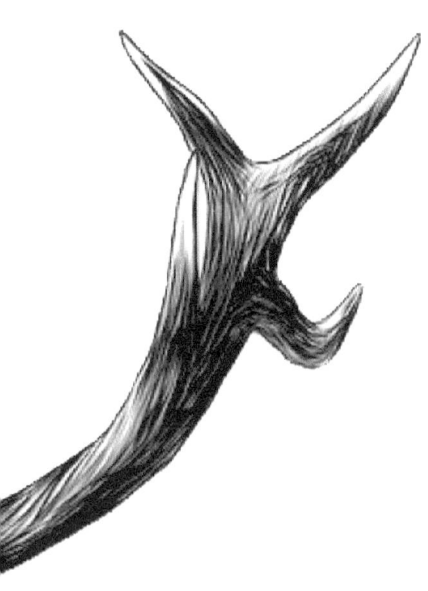

DEER

TAURUS MOON, LIBRA SUN, SANDHILL CRANES

The Sandhill Cranes returned
the day she learned she had MS

She dipped her cedar kayak paddle
into the water

looked at her reflection
thought of Narcissus

She bought a bouquet of autumn flowers
at the Saturday Farmer's Market

names of autumn flowers remembered
Asters, Black-eyed Susans, Chrysanthemums,

she made a cup of Sumatra coffee
thick, black, global realities swirling around her

of course, she always ate splendidly
lots of cruciferous vegetables

brussel sprouts, cauliflower, broccoli,
daily visualizing wellness

yes, she exercised every day, the lament of
preventative health care turned inside out

cadmium red facial feathers on the cranes
flight feathers a luminous gray

not black or white, not artificial
positive thinking, positive PH in the water

acupuncture needles carefully placed, sensations, *Teh Chi*
along meridians, flowers like common Sneezeweeds

as a child she lived ten, fifty miles away
from the Hanford Nuclear Plant

the government said there was no connection
with the increase in glioblastomas, MS, autoimmune disorders,

cancer in Camas, Washougal, the Columbia River Watershed
and the leaching of chemicals into the water

Plutonium, Beryllium, liquid wastes, radioactive debris
plus *Round-up*® all around the beautiful fall flowers

the Sioux and Cheyenne used Swan, Hawk and Crane feathers
in their headdresses, gifted Golden Eagle feathers

as a child she watched the Grand Entrance at the rodeo
Pendleton Round-Up

She lays the old wool blankets
on her red cherrywood sleigh bed

Star Watchers, Painted Hills, Falcon Cove
Big Medicine, she sleeps with her medicine bundle

listens to the Night Hawk, White-tailed Deer
wind in the Red Cedar, Sandhill Cranes overhead

Autumn migration, gratitude
returning.

Snow Geese, Telemetry, *PTSD*

Flocks of Snow Geese overhead,
along with Dusky Geese, Canadian Geese.
Disrupted, the birds move like the electrical activity
across the telemetry screen,
then the single screen firearms simulator.

She has an arrhythmia, post-chemo, post traumatic stress disorder,
post-relocation, post-election, post-war.
Chai, one of the Thai elephants from the Woodland Park Zoo,
died one hundred miles from Broken Arrow, the Trail of Tears.

Tornadoes in the high plains in November.
then in Battleground, Washington in December.
She ran five miles amongst pastures and prairie
every winter morning when she lived in Selah.

She dreams of owning horses, donkeys, llamas.
In Pakistan, Syria, Kenya, Beirut and France
she sees the children's faces, bloodied,
more civilians killed than soldiers.

A passenger jet, a train, a trolley, a boat blown up
unnamed borderlands around the world
daily reminders of war, fracking, oil spills, walls,
poverty spilling out across lines of water rights.

Her neighbor shoots the raccoon family
that forges in the spaces between
the Western Red Cedar and the Sword Ferns
that mark the property line between them.

She hears the Mama crying.
She has taken the pain
of the world
into her heart.

FUSED GLASS, MEMORIES

Swirls of gold, cerulean blue
She is touching her beauty, she is crying

softened by mosses, rain, yellow cedar
how to breathe, how to heal herself again and again

the trumpet-bell shaped flowers, vines green in the background
shimmer of light, crow

you cannot get lost when you hold it
Crow drinks out of the fountain

Softened by mosses, rain, yellow cedar
how to breathe, how to heal herself again and again

listening at the gates of her heart, she asks her winged guardians
for assistance   there is turquoise in the center of her breath

you cannot get lost when you hold it
Crow drinks out of the fountain

listening to the sky, her heart   kestrel overhead
They look like olive trees, not here   a distant country

listening at the gates of her heart, she asksher winged guardians
for assistance   there is turquoise in the center of her breath

you cannot get lost when you hold it
Crow drinks out of the fountain

listening to the sky, her heart   kestrel overhead
They look like olive trees, not here   a distant country

Swirls of gold, cerulean blue
She is touching her beauty, she is crying.

DIURNAL RAPTORS

What do the birds of prey have to tell you?
Pause   feel the wind in your tail feathers
Red-tailed Hawk carries your morning prayers
from earth to heaven,
like Golden Eagle, holding a higher perspective
numinous in the sheen of rain, sun-lit.

Look carefully at the letter shapes
of your life,
your intentions
the vowels and consonants
Accipiters, Buteos, Falcons, Harriers.
Prayers of intercessions
have similar postures.

Write on damp clay tablets
so mistakes may be
easily smoothed out,
conversations and requests noted
like little white field mice
scurrying underneath
the winter wheat.

Kestrel comes from another
direction, a diagonal line.
landing on a Douglas Fir limb
which slopes to the earth
as an incantation.

Wing your way through
the sorrow,
lift your wings in gratitude.

SHE DREAMS IN ARABIC

"The Moon nuzzles its way into comforting Cancer,
where attention turns to our emotional needs.
Feelings become more important than facts."

    –LEAH WHITEHORSE, Astrologer[2]

Waking at four o'clock in the morning
the day after Thanksgiving
she dreams in Arabic
the back yard still moon-lit

Raccoons eating birdseed
squabbles near the bird bath
three Great Horned Owls
illuminate the starry sky.

She refuses to turn on the computer
go to a store, go anywhere.
When did *Fur Free Friday*
become *Black Friday*?

When did a day of gratitude be hallowed
by a day of greed?
She walks before the sun rises,
greeted by Barred Owl.

Rose Hips bright red, round
like rosary beads or mala beads.
She gathered with Muslims, Baha'i,
Native Americans, Episcopalians, Jews,

New Thought, Methodist, Catholic,
Pagan Sisters and Brothers
Thanksgiving Eve service
everyone sang, prayed, ate together,

honoring gratitude, praying for peace.
The Christians forgot and brought pork and non-kosher food
no one said anything, though she thought
of course it was the Christians

like the Americans in Istanbul
drinking hot tea and arguing over the price
of rugs hand-tied by children.
They forgot. We forget.

She forgot to leave carrots out for the Eastern Cottontail Rabbits
and four were hopping around the yard, waiting when she
returned from her walk.
Even the raccoons looked into the picture window, expectant.
She bows to the birds and animals.

She sees children in West African
waiting for Jollof Rice, Fufu, Peanut Stew.
They have been waiting since she lived there three decades ago.
Military jets fly too low. The Grey Squirrel freezes. Everyone freezes
as if there is a Cooper's Hawk
or Barred Owl in the Japanese Maple again.

Once she knew how to write and speak simple sentences
in several languages. She has forgotten so much. We have forgotten.
The borders are opened and closed again. Refugees are dying.
A tornado goes past the local bakery
while the owner was making cinnamon rolls.

When she bikes to work the next day,
she talks to the woman living in her car with her cats.
She has a large bag of cat food
and a loaf of homemade bread in the seat.
A lone coyote walks across deer meadow,
pausing in the frozen stubble
of burdock and winter wheat glazed by hoar frost.

She calls to it without opening her mouth.
The coyote turns slightly toward her, listening for voles.
The woman bends down to look at bird tracks,
Italic letters in the frozen mud and ice.
A half dozen Cormorants fly high overhead, black wings on violet-blue.

As in her dream, she wraps a *hijab* around her head,
wears a long skirt, walks the streets of Istanbul and Damascus
the woman who is homeless is walking with her cats
the Turkish women invite them in for tea.

MAY WE LISTEN

I believe in listening to the white-breasted nuthatch
the song of the houseless, homeless man
singing outside his brick-red burnt-red REI tent
pitched along the creekside, miles from Yacolt
he sings constellations we have forgotten the names of

Long ago our ancestors
also dreamt under the starry sky,
spinning rainbows, salmon light in the water
First Nations, refugees, immigrants, indigenous
Poetry Moves on C-Tran Express Bus

Do that which brings you joy he says,
honor civility, equity, inclusion
listen to the many languages of the Pacific tree frog,
brilliant yellow-green on the long arms of skunk cabbage
not far from Ridgefield Wildlife Refuge.

The chorus frogs, violin, cello, cicadas, Ghost Town poets,
wind in the cottonwood trees, Vancouver Symphony
Autumn leaves a seasonal palette, changing again after the
Washougal Arts Festival, Camas Arts Festival.

The white-tailed deer return to her backyard each morning
gingerly stepping over small animal burrows
honey bees on white clover, blackberries ripening
the doe can hear the man who is houseless, a tenor
his voice rises with the wind, like a rapper
or drums from a rock band at the Clark County Fairground

A Latina walks past him, born in the USA,
Flamingo pink headset tuned to 94.3 *La Zeta!*
Buenos dias! Her *hermano* painting on a canvas in Guadalajara
before he goes to work teaching *turistos Español.*
Her daughter writing a poem in Camas, English class
The ruby-crowned Kinglet sings a small *kwee kwee*

Your neighbor who is in treatment has a green chemo headwrap
the color of kinglet feathers,
her heartbeat the sound of the Salish drum
we hear hoof beats of the Buffalo Soldiers in the distance

May we dip our paddles in the water,
listen closely when she speaks.
Star-lit beyond the clouds
Great Egrets flying, luminous, we listen.

Omnivorous

(Tamias Townsendil
Rodentia Sciuridae)[1]

Here's a hint: look at her face
basic brown
with a clearly defined dark stripe
stretching from nose to eye
five dark, four cinnamon-brown stripes.
She is a storer of wisdom, insect wings
gathering seeds in her cheek pouches
caching them, thousands of seeds
conifer seeds, thistle seeds
maples seeds, gnosis, ten thousand wishes.
She likes Salal berries, Blackberries, Thimbleberries
roots, fruit and fungi
spreading the spores of mushrooms
around the forest floor with her feet.
Field Note: She is diurnal, territorial
vocalizes frequently
chirp, trill, chuck notes
inquisitive, yet shy
even as she sits on the deck

of Elderberry Cabin
small head slightly turned
toward meadow grasses, Red Alder Leaves,
Yellow Cedar, the sea and the moon.

SHE ASKED THE TREES TO PRAY FOR US

The White-tailed doe and her fawns greet us at dawn.
We didn't know our neighbors would cut down
the 120' Hemlock, Grandfather,
the boundary tree on the West property line
and the Douglas Fir, Red Cedar, Japanese Maple
that protected our home too.

"Hey, Nigger!" last night at First Friday Art Walk,
as we crossed the street, climbed into our Raven-black truck.
My spouse stunned, my feelings tasered.   I freeze, hands down.
Downtown Vancouver across from the Clark County Court House,
seven blocks from where our Latino friend was assaulted.
"Hey, Nigger! Hey, Nigger!"
this past year of electoral college reneging.

Her father cannot remember his address anymore.
His wife of twenty-five years
asked for a respite when she had surgery,
never says goodbye, sends divorce papers via her son.
Her father cannot remember
he signed a second mortgage, other papers
giving away many of his rights to her family
a month after his last stroke.   In sickness and in health.

Vascular dementia, the vascular cambium of the tree
concentric circles, pith, heartwood,
the vascular tissue conducts light,
the neighborhood smells like freshly cut fir, cedar.
Our roof is covered in hemlock-white saw dust.
The stump has a 45" diameter.
The Hummingbirds, the Crows,
and Ruby-crowned Kinglet lost their homes.
Her father does not know he will never see his home again.

The white men at the bus stop repeat "Hey, Nigger!"
I glare as we drive away, think I should tell the gallery owner.
The sun shines through our living room window;
we have lost our privacy.
"Oh! You will have more daylight!" a friend aims to be optimistic.
We have never needed air conditioning, a fence, visceral protection.
We had our hemlock, cedar, maple, canopy of trees, family trust.

CROW FINDS WHAT YOU WERE LOOKING FOR

The white sage stick gifted to you
in Wolf Creek, Montana
gratitude   lost Neruda poems
an astrological chart completed
for your twenty-first birthday
a quote by Starhawk
another by Pierre Teilhard de Chardin
both written on pieces of handmade paper
from Nepal   your fifth-grade band book
ten years of forgiveness of well-meaning adults
tea tree and lemon flower balm
a ribbon from a half marathon, a lucky rabbit's foot
air miles, a bus ticket to Vancouver, British Columbia
silver quarters gifted to you by your great uncle
the announcement for an interfaith peace walk
your "know your numbers"
(including your blood pressure)
a group-on for dance lessons, voice lessons, a massage
your grandmother's recipes for sweet potato pie
fried ochre and corn fritters
a Spanish textbook from your freshman year

a map to Willapa National Wildlife Refuge walking trail
a small brown button   your old car keys
dream fragments from the night before last

kaw! kaw! kaw!
a flash of shiny black wings
seven crows fly East from the Cedar tree
they have something in their beaks.

RABBIT

FOUND OBJECT

–for my grandmother Ina

Burgundy flowers, English motif
tole-painted on her writing desk
the one that faced East
pushed up against the window
with a hard swivel chair also tole-painted
she let me sit in it when
I visited, allowed me to open her
small brown boxes of buttons, stamps,
paper clips, memories, found objects.

She drew patterns of
wild roses, birds, paisley designs
on thin tissue paper
now yellowed in manila folders
in my filing cabinet
each image founds its way
on a new ceramic piece
rabbit, sparrow, rose,
a handmade card.

She taught art classes in
a small studio with tables
allowed me to sit quietly
in the back or move to the writer's desk
to scribble my own designs or drawings.
"Oh! How sweet your granddaughter is here!"
I wanted Midge
her black and tan dachshund to sit with me
yet the dog wanted to be as close to my grandmother as possible.

That was before "john doe" started to court her,
lure her away from her art
with the promise of horses,
a home in the country,
a place for a larger studio
he then never allowed.
The grief silenced her.
The writing desk was moved after he died
chipped on the edges. Things weren't talked about.
Her kilns and art supplies
had disappeared with her warm smile.

She told me she wanted to
paint more flowers,
tried to quilt again,

made me a hand tied rug
that I kept in the back of my truck for years
white and blue flowers
like forget-me-nots.

The Palomino she called "Hope"
used to come to the wooden gate, waiting for me
to bring apples.

I remember her as she sat at her writing desk,
eyes happy, then sad, watching the rain.

GARDNERSVILLE ESTATE, JOLOF RICE
(Liberia, West Africa)

Jolof Rice, Palm Butter, Fried Plantain
she touched the wooden spoon to her lip
dropped it to the cooking pot
hugged us close, "Oh Thank God you're home!"

Together we took faded red cotton rags
soaked in warm water, salt
and cleaned Gabriel's wounds
where the soldiers had whipped him.

Braided scars across his black skin
songs of freedom, songs of grief
"By the Rivers of Babylon"
the West African rendition.

Fizzle of Orange Crush®, Coca Cola®
Gabriel told us the story
how the President ordered soldiers
to the University,

African, Green Beret, CIA-backed units.
We ate Palm Butter Rice, fried spam,
plantain, listened, "and there we wept"
plume of Ibis, plume of smoke

American tanks rolled, our friends, classmates
shot, whipped, raped, disappeared.
"Where's Mary?" she whispered
crumpled bodies in the back of the truck.

This morning we walk along Salmon Creek
water dark, swollen like the bellies
of our friends, parallel lines of sticks, stones
stories, repeated histories

a young black man lynched this winter
outside of Everett. We cook
Jolof Rice, with carrots and peas,
Muslim, Jew, Christian, Pagan,

we pass the wooden spoon
hand to hand with
our braided stories of survival.
Where will we bury our dead?

"PUTTING THE DAMAGE ON"
—for Tori Amos

Wayfaring, aeropress office
in Inverness above the sea
she adds a dollop of cream
the color of sheep wool

sends a photo of Dava Moor
ten o'clock in the evening on Summer Solstice
the sun never setting
at that latitude, longitude

the sweet cube of sugar
the bruises the color of coffee beans
then French lavender, fresh
bunches of dried lavender

her sorrow penned into a postcard
watercolor of Highland Heather
a cropping of stones, Celtic Crosses
she wanders along the valley

her despair rings like sheep bells,
cow bells, church bells

melodic, yet shimmering
like summer sunlight, the sound of the bells

the arch of the blue sky filled with clouds
like the cream in her coffee
spin drift, the skiff in the water
the sea birds she didn't know the names of

except for the Puffins, orange beaks
Orange Oolong tea in a small black kettle
not from China, grave markers of the wars
before at every crossing

wayfaring souls,
ancestors, descendants. She walks
the emerald isle in a long green tunic
knapsack, rucksack filled

resentments, forgiveness, family fluids
disputed arguments, lines of reason,
ley lines, the circle of the Celtic Knots, infinity
the bells, hammer dulcimer, harpsichord

music of damaged lives, coffee ground scattered on the garden,
pea pods, tomato plants, zucchini,

she writes a poem about a victim
who killed herself in the church bathroom

chose/did not choose to exit via suicide
Tori sang about this a decade
before it happened, just before
just after Holy Week, the crosses covered in Lenten shrouds

her voice covered by domestic violence, ecclesial violence
she walked the perimeter of the church,
the narthex, up to the altar,
someone said she had taken communion the day before

bread for the journey, the last rite
sparkling lemon water, grape juice, red wine, communion wine
she walks along the edge of the cemetery
says she sees ghosts

tendrils of spirits like climbing roses,
pink roses, luminous remembrances
write a poem about a victim
who was shot in the head

execution style by her husband
under the St. John's Bridge
write a poem about the man
who shot himself beside his girlfriend

after the concert, listening to lyrics,
Don't go walking down Suicide Alley, she sang
she walked the perimeter of her dreams,
her despair, drinking coffee

French press, espresso ground
from Kenya or Guatemala or South Africa
she wore a long skirt, a gold band,
sorrow, her hem dragging on the green earth

the clouds shaped like Fjord ponies,
the clumps of sugar in the sugar bowl.

SATURN SEXTILE PALLAS

One day after the Full Moon in Sagittarius
writing post-London Bridge, no. 45
bees wax, genocide, Magpie wings
black on white, white on black
record album: vinyl, digital
recording spirituals, angels
cherubim, seraphim, archangel
white wings, black wings
gilded in illuminated politics
she carries rose quartz in her pocket
plays her pocket flute
talks to the Magpie, the messenger
in the center of this moment
Sagittarius Moon, round as a communion wafer,
illuminated host rising over the Coastal Hills
this wasn't supposed to happen
history repeating
like a vinyl album, needle sticking
on sugar cubes, rock salt, pepper corn
black on white, white on black.

We are slow to listen
to cosmic messengers, Raven, Magpie

King, Brown, Walker, Tubman
circles of obituaries, circles of light
from the police officer's flashlight
he/she/they/we still carry
rounds of metal, rounds of bullets
embedded in her brother's chest
white wings, black wings
gilded in illuminated politics
alternative facts, sorrow on fire
she plays the album backwards
no. 45 not 666
revelations carved into the White Oak tree
the cedar park bench
we knock on wood
invoke the spirit of the trees
angels gathered, writing postmortem
post-grief, post-herstory
that wasn't written
crystallized rose quartz
the stars around Our Lady of Guadalupe
hand-painted on her turban, hijab, roses, stars
black on white, white on black
the Magpie flies from the cedar to the fir
talks to her, the tree,
the angels of her relatives, tree brown

this is what she meant to tell you
picking up another flight feather, another promise
falsetto of politico, ponderosa puzzle pieces
sweet pine, sweet chariot
sweet tea, sweet potato pie
the crust round as the Moon
in Sagittarius, full
the Archer bends her bow strings
post no. 45
aims for the stars.

Involuntary Departure, Cyrillic Alphabet

She was wrapped in a shroud, black and gold
buried amidst earthen prayers, red roses
DV: Domestic Violence
VAWA: the Violence Against Women Act
it is hard to know
how to write, paint, read
take care of the sick, the lonely, the dead
take public transport down alphabet streets
sort through alphabet visas.
Did you know about the U Visa?

She had a US Visa
was from Bosnia, a town of many letters
prayers, letters, spilled out with tea leaves
when the Bosnian Imam
turned toward us, the women
wind blowing cold from the East
hajib, head-covered women,
he said in broken English,
"I am sorry," he said
what it meant to return to the earth.
Her children, whose names begin

with the first letter of the alphabet
Cyrillic or English, Hebrew or Greek,
stood before us, orphaned.
She was wrapped in the sorrow
of her friends, our tears,
of a rainbow arching over the minarets of trees
beyond the cemetery
the alphabet in shapes of sticks, stones, runes,
unknown heritages.

When blood drips from her hands
into the carpet of their home
Carpe diem, seize the day
was her unsung credo.
You may get a U Visa when you are
a victim of crime,
a victim of removal proceedings,
postpartum, postmortem, deportation.
Did you know the closest
detention center is in Steilacoom?
Owned by the Geo Group,
a private contractor,
international, like letters

stories, words, alphabet soup
sensitive locations policy
legal right to not disclose.

She was wrapped in a
shroud of silence.

VOICES, FEATHERS, MINARETS

One lone Tundra Swan
circles over the Western Red Cedars, cries.
This is how we start.

A mother deported from Phoenix,
her fourteen-year-old daughter, cries,
"It's not right to have to pack
a suitcase for your mother."
Undocumented, Latina, here, working for 21 years
paying taxes, social security, school fees
no documents her only offense, before the defense attorney
building the fence, we break down.

The Tundra Swan, cries.
Keep writing about this,
don't lose your flock, your tribe, your people.
My spouse called "Nigger" again, no, again and again.

At the mosque
the Imam gathers his brothers
Friday prayer
the white feather of the swan
the white prayer rug

the white papers
which determine her removal
my sister, my brother, it is "removal" now, not deportation.

It is the dreamers who are speaking out for DACA
because they have their white papers today
today, when we have a safety plan
our neighbor from Cuba plays his drums quietly

how he pounds on our African djembe.
We walk past a flock of Snow Geese, Canada Geese
returning from the South, no atmospheric wall between
artificial boundaries
Spring migration, the birds begin to return
from South America
white wing feathers, flight feathers
tall minarets. This is how we start.

At the synagogue the Rabbi gathers her people
for Friday prayer.
The white feather of the Swan
the white scroll of the Torah, the Q'uran
a mother deported from Phoenix, from your neighborhood.
What is rising from the ashes of hate and despair?
Who is rising, speaking?

Cattle Egret, Great Egret
gather along the edge of the water
talking to us in another language.
*The Language of Birds*³ comes from sacred texts.
This is how we start.

RIVER OTTERS, SALMON CREEK

The day after Autumn Equinox
a family of five river otters reappear
one whistles, I whistle back

Three heads pop out of the water
Otter looking at me
O! whistle while you work

A young man is whistling, carrying a cage, a trap
I freeze like the thistle, teasel,
brown burdock on the bank

the otters disappear
like a change of consciousness
a change of conscience

it could be who is trapping the beaver
illegal as the deportation of our sisters and brothers
Latinx, Sikh, immigrant, refugee, almost citizen

caging of children, separating parent from child,
trapping of women's experience, stage set
whistling of politicians, red violations

our neighbor finds two beavers,
skinned on the bank near his house
nothing in this situation prepared us for this

moral distress, lunar shift, voter shift
the young man shifts when I ask
"What are you doing?!"

his buddy appears, shifts, looks toward the water
I imagine the otters are my witness
hiding behind stalks of cattails

recording our conversation
then smacking my fear like trout on the river-stones
sticks and stones, bones, court rooms

red ties, blue ties, fly fishing ties
electronic surveillance, skeletons in the closet
a buzz of flies, drones, voices

Her voice, "I shall resist,"
the River Otter whistles again.

WE RESIST BY FORGETTING

Two Stellar Jays land phthalo blue on the sap green bird feeder
mid-summer, mid-life, mid-year election

we forget what day it is, what year it is
the names of women we have known for years

the days of being left alone as a child, pre-teen
childhood ACE scores not as high as yours

rabbits eat clover, gray squirrels dig, bury sunflower seeds
the holes of our conscious, ethics

women who have been violated
children who have been disappeared

survivors vilified, violators honored
drama-trauma nation

pseudo-democratic fascism
disciplined alcoholic misogyny

incivility, O! the moral compass spins
as if we were in The Trump Triangle

we lose our bearings, bureaucracy, decency
a flock of Mourning Doves arrive

the Cooper's Hawk screams through the yard
and everyone scatters below the fighter jets

our thoughts lost in
daily disruption of unwellness

children in cages, parents in detention
("it's like summer camp" chimes the newscaster)

clock tower chimes, church chimes, doorbell chimes
what hour of conscientious objection?

I draw flowers with crayons, beeswax
paint over with watercolor, simple designs

wax resistance, war resistance
malware, spyware, data breach

Big brother knows what we are doing even when
she places a blue-green sticky note over the camera of your lap top

desk top; do not blame Bulgaria, Canada, China, Russia, your cousin,
blue counter top, toy top, the Stellar Jays return

squawking *Blue! Blue! Blue! Vote! Vote! Vote!*
every day she signs an electronic petition, a written petition

regarding some national affliction
degradation of human rights, environmental rights, civil rights

slaughter of wolves, waters, bees, children, ethics
she starts a list of all undocumented persons killed by ICE

police or persons who forgot who they were
mental health, mental illness, national illness, border militia

she writes on the calendar every day her black friends
are harassed on the road, daily DWB (driving while black)

the brown rabbits hop straight into the deer herd
play games in the stretch of meadow grass

where are the children?
she can't find her lists, can't find her keys, can't find her children

your father living with Alzheimer's disease, vascular dementia
can't remember the name of his address, children, the dogwood tree

white glue, wood glue, what is holding our nation together?
she writes a poem, draws with eyebrow pencil above your moral distress

crayon resist, she draws
with a white crayon on black paper

black crayon on white paper
wax resist is a waxy substance used to prevent

glazes from adhering onto the clay body
under glazes of lost memory, history, herstory, her body
she resists.

OWL

16 APRIL, *EN TREN, BUENOS DIAS*

6:00 a.m. 39 degrees Fahrenheit
the train follows the Klamath River
winding, Coffee Creek,
Dunsmuir, Coast Starlight train.
I follow the river with conifer trees,
ponderosa pine and weeping willow
apple and pear,
early spring flowers in bloom
buttercup, columbine, and mule's ears
a sunrise view of Mt. Shasta
before the fires burned with our fury.

I carry a soft leather satchel,
the hope, sadness and grief
of my father and his father
who died at my age
weep with my brothers
as a small kestrel flies over the train.
This morning, earlier,
I woke hearing
Great Horned Owl
when the trained stopped
in the woods

the same place
where all afternoon
the rabbits had gathered.

Roman, the train attendant,
offers us coffee,
"hot, fresh, from Colombia
just like me…"
the passion of the world
held in a white coffee cup
compass pointed north
with the presence of our ancestors
many languages spoken
amidst sage brush
sorrow, morning sun,
a trio of mule deer.

ODE TO THE BARRED OWL

Who comes swooping through our yard
over the brambles of indigenous blackberries,
Sword Ferns, feral zucchini, Trillium,
the Eastern Cottontail who was eating baby carrots and bird seed
dives into the thickets, down into the earth
like a dreamer hurrying into archetypal night visions.

Owl, harbinger of death, life, light unto light,
white feathers like Barn Owl, Snowy Owl, dream owls
the carved white soapstone owl of the Inuit, Yup'ik,
silent messenger, the owl turns, flies from
the Japanese Maple to the Western Red Cedar and back again.

Our neighbor comes out on her back deck in a white terry-cloth robe
her feathers ruffled in the early dawn
after too many glasses of "Mystery Pour"
at *Niche* wine bar the night before.
What is the koan this owl bears in its flight feathers?
Messages across centuries, myths, urban legends.

She said she heard the owl calling before her brother
died in Afghanistan. "He didn't belong there," she said.
I assumed her brother, not the owl.

Barred Owl, taking the territory of other owls,
like we, the Americans, in history, her story.

I see Spotted Owls, Great Horned Owls
 in the trees above our tomato plants.
Cutesy owls appear on Valentine candy made in China.
The Salish man who carved a Raven figure in Nanaimo
glared at my partner, turned from her in the studio
when she asked if there were any owl carvings.
An elder had warned us that owls are seen as unwelcome omens.

In that part of British Columbia, owls,
and things like war and addiction
not spoken of in the company of strangers or at a garden party.
In the part of West Africa where my partner assumes her ancestry,
there are Eagle Owls, large birds of prey who dominate the landscape.
We watch the Owl who makes daily visits in our back yard.

In the morning, before the sun rises, before repeated rumors of rain,
random shootings, foreclosures, extreme weather, earthquakes,
we recall our dreams while drinking coffee
from the highlands of Guatemala.
The owl flies silently over the Italian Basil, over the damp earth.

PLUTO CROSSES THE ECLIPTIC

Uncertainty, Screech Owl, Little Brown Creeper
the brown on brown of owl on cedar limb

little passerine hitching upward
spiraling around tree trunk of morning news

in the morning we gather rain boots, jackets, petitions,
astrological charts, field guides to the birds and stars

the language of the Loon is the memory of our ancestors
black on white, white on black, tremolo call

coastal and inward waters, emotions,
radiation from Fukashima Daiichi illuminating the Salish Sea

the Strait of Juan de Fuca, wintering birds
media propaganda, swirling with false news

Washington State stands up against the current administration
the only known place where Common Loons overwinter

saltwater, freshwater, how we taste truth and lies in our mouths
how Pluto Crosses the Ecliptic, following a lunar shift, political shift

armed with an underworld torch, we go further
and deeper still into the depths, oppositions

how the Owl moves across the woodlands
how the Loon calls across the saltwater

how the ancestors warn our descendants about our fishing choices
shad, alewife, trout, mudminnows, sticklebacks and walleye

how we remember, forget, remember again
planets, celestials, feathers guiding us back home.

An indulgence

Three deer come to their bird feeder each morning
to graze on red millet, black-oiled sunflowers, wild bird seed
she watches the chickadees wait, impatient as her neighbor
waiting for a phone call from her sister in Puerto Rico
post-hurricane, waiting to hear the phone ring,
hear the oven timer go off,
know that her frittata is done, her family okay.
The deer push the feeder with their legs, hooves against metal
she drinks *Genmaicha,* melts a square
 of Mount Shasta dark chocolate in her mouth,
remembers her September dreams, animals on the ridge,
traveling in South America. She has forgotten her passport.
The next dream everyone is evacuating, North Korea bombing
San Francisco, the West Coast, transition, jump-cut in her dream.
Fragments when that night, out of the blue, in waking
a transgender professional in Boise
receives three texts in rapid succession:
"it is legal to discriminate against bad behavior in Idaho."
It is Friday night in waking, the week before her neighbor,
drinking on his porch with his bodies, shouts at them "Homos!"
She tells her friends she wanted to shout back,
"At least get your language right!"
Politically incorrect bullying.

Indulgence of chocolate, safety, half-closed dreams
scribed at waking between sips of green tea.
Chiron retrogrades into a sextile with Juno, enabling everyone to
find a fix for problems with agreements earlier in the months.
Her neighbor, her brother, both drink beer every night,
carry concealed weapons, or shotguns in the pick-up truck gun rack.
The last time she visited the Sawtooth Mountains she rode horses
all day with her adopted niece.
An Appaloosa named Arthur carried her up
the mountain trail toward the snow caps.
Burnt umber leather saddle on titanium white, dappled gray
the horse indulged her by going carefully under the Pine trees
so the branches wouldn't hit her face
she stopped to dig squares of chocolate and almonds,
out of her pockets, sip tea from the thermos,
watch coyotes, deer in the meadow,
sunlight filtered through threats, sorrow, alder leaves.

BERGAMOT, LLAMAS, RAIN

We have walked here in the rain
to drink tea, gather words, italic letters

a pair of Varied Thrush
plumage pumpkin orange
a homeless man
with a handmade cart

attached to his bicycle
under a blue tarp in the woods
a mile from here
the raccoons gather, the white-tailed deer

waiting for me to fill up the bird feeders
"don't feed raccoons!"
"don't give money to the homeless!"
words of seasoned social workers

the llamas spit at the visitors
I fill up the bird bath with water
it will rain tomorrow
the raccoons sleep on top

of the ivy-covered tree stump, 40' high
huddled close to one another
six stellar jays, complementary colors
bright blue feathers again the orange thrush

we love words mid-life, post-chemo, post-menopausal
loss of estrogen, elasticity,

loss of hair, memory, breath
we have walked here in the rain.

"AND ALL RAIN IS HOLY WATER" SHE SAYS[4]

three raccoons came to the bird feeder this morning
before she had her first cup of hibiscus tea
before it started raining
a woman was taken off a TriMet bus[5]
yesterday by ICE[6]
on her way to work, she was late
she is in the detention center in Tacoma
her children in custody in Portland
it is raining between them
the fog rises from the Columbia River
a Great Blue Heron lifts her wings
rises along the mud flats
her family in *Oaxaca, Otavalo*
her family in Rose City Park
her family in detention
her family in deportation proceedings.

She fingers the rosary in her pocket
Our Lady of Guadalupe
Rosewood prayers
"I will never forget you"
she says to her children, *niños*
segregated by fear

immigration regulations
she cannot see the clouds
behind the wall
the gray edges of sorrow
remembers the flight feathers of the heron
the silver chain of the rosary
rosewood, rose water
the deer eat the wild roses in the backyard
a doe, two fawns, black-tailed
she will be black-listed
is black listed, dreams of the three sisters
black beans, corn, delicata candy stripe squash.

Her daughter has roses on her rain boots,
splashes in puddles, sings the alphabet song
in English, in Spanish, waiting for the no. 2 bus
dreaming, she walks through the waters
of the Rio Grande again
raccoons gather at the river
"and all rain is holy water" she says.

ENDNOTES

1. S.K. Headley and S. Sells, Townsend's Chipmunk *Tamias townsendii*,Oregon State University extension Catalog EC 1580 • December 2005

2. Leah Whitehorse: Lua Astrology, www.leahwhitehorse.com

3. The Language of Birds, *The Sacred Q'uran*

4. Terry Dicks, poet reading: http://www.npr.org/sections/healthshots/2017/02/20/514558968/can-poetry-keep-you-young-science-is-still-out-but-the-heart-says-yes

5. With almost 80 lines, TriMet buses serve much of the Portland, Oregon Metro area

6. ICE, Immigration and Customs Enforcement

ACKNOWLEDGMENTS

With gratitude to Connor Wolfe, editor and publisher of Homebound Publications, as well as the following publications and organizations in which these poems have previously been honored or printed, sometimes in slightly different forms.

Clark County Arts Commission, Poet Laureate Inauguration: May We Listen, Credo for the first day of Clark County Poet Laureate no.2

Poetry Moves—Arts of Clark County, (Artstra), Clark County Arts Commission, C-Tran, Printed Matter, Vancouver: Hope Embossed

129+ : More Poets of Washington: Snow Geese, Telemetry, PTSD

Wayfarer: And All Rain is Holy Water; Involuntary Departure, Cyrillic Alphabet; Voices, Feathers, Minarets

Willamette Writers, Kay Snow Paulann Petersen Poetry Prize, 3rd place 2017: Seven Mourning Doves

Willamette Writers, Paulann Petersen Poetry Prize, 3rd place, 2018: "and all rain is holy water," she says

Written River: Omnivorous

With gratitude to my beloved Judy A. Rose, our friends and family, colleagues and *compañeras* for their love and support. With honor to all the thousands of people living with cancer and autoimmune disorders linked to environmental toxins, and to the earth for holding our pain. *Namaste* to many artists, chaplains, dreamers, holistic practitioners, musicians, poets and writers who have provided critique, encouragement and inspiration. Gratitude to Peter Boehlke, Patrish Pearce, Victoria Stein, Dawn Thompson and Karen Wood for holding a vision of creativity over the years. Much gratitude to Joan Borysenko, Jason Kirkey, John Fox, Sandra Ingerman, Mariana Romo-Carmona, Kim Stafford, Chase Twichell and writers who have provided support to me and many poets and writers. Thank you to Scott Franz of FrugalNavigator. com for providing topographic map. Thanks to Michael Lerner, Francis Weller and Commonweal staff for creating healing spaces. Appreciation to the Sitka Center for Art and Ecology in Otis, Oregon and Leah Jackson, Angst Gallery, Vancouver. Enormous gratitude to LaRae Zawodny and the Clark County Arts Commission for honoring me with the title of Clark County Poet Laureate, following in the steps of Christopher Luna and his spouse Toni Lumbrazo Luna, publishers at Printed Matter and mentors for many poets and writers in Washington State. Thanks to Stephanie Austin and Leah Whitehorse for gifting us with wisdom of astrologic insights every lunar cycle. With gratitude to all the kindred spirits of Lavender Dreams Farm and Donkey Rescue as well as other animal rescue organizations. In honor of all the poets, writers, artists and musicians who are holding up the light of their artistic gifts for the healing of this world. This book emerged with the care of our larger community as well as the support of all our ancestors, angels, helping spirits and guides.

Special thanks to Susan Bourdet for the gift of "Emerald Lake," the watercolor of Loons gracing the cover of this book.

Mitakuye Oyasin – "We are all related."

About the Author

Gwendolyn Morgan learned the names of birds and wildflowers and inherited paintbrushes and boxes from her grandmothers. With an M.F.A. in Creative Writing from Goddard College, and an M.Div. from San Francisco Theological Seminary and the Graduate Theological Union, she has been a recipient of artist and writing residencies at Artsmith, Caldera, Into the Depths of Winter, and Soapstone. *Crow Feathers, Red Ochre, Green Tea,* her first book of poems, was a winner of the Wild Earth Poetry Prize, Hiraeth Press. *Snowy Owls, Egrets and Unexpected Graces* (initially published by Hiraeth Press and currently published by Homebound Publications) is a Nautilus Gold Winner in Poetry and a *Foreword Review* Indies Book of the Year Finalist in the Nature Category. Her poems have appeared in: *Calyx, Kalliope, Mudfish, Tributaries: A Journal of Nature Writing, Wayfarer, Written River* as well as *The Cancer Poetry Project 2*, and other anthologies, blogs, and literary journals. She is the Clark County Poet Laureate 2018-2020 in Washington State. Gwendolyn and Judy A. Rose, her spouse, share their home, music and creekside walks with Naomi, a rescued Cardigan Corgi & Chesapeake Retriever mix.